AHSAASMERA

A SUMMARY OF A GLOBETROTTER

SAKET KUMAR

Contents

Ahsaasmera

Today I will be silent, but my soul will speak about an incident which is worth a story of hardness, embarrassment and curse. A story which inconclusively took the beautiful life into a deadly hell of sorrows. A simple story of a selfless person with a magnanimous heart, true to his deeds and understood this world of truth and falsehood. But someone has rightly said the good things spoil due to an evil eye, the same happened with his course of life too. There came a dramatic change in his life...... The love with her voice, her smile, her glimpse which continuously provoked him to take her into his dreamy expectations but couldn't as if it was kept in a 2 inched tightly glass cased packed inside a museum providing the visitors the only privilege to spectate the beauty. But the love for her made him blind. His instinct relentlessly called forth for his approach but he couldn't. But there is a factor which comes play role here, that is friends, our boon companions. They insisted him, ignited his courage and made him realised with the fact of "Yathartha", that is truth. The thing which lord Krishna has scripted to be happened in this world, that will only happen we are just the puppets of the drama, the ideas still reside with the puppeteer i.e., Lord Krishna. We need not to think of outcomes before doing, it goes pointless.

Then he spent his whole night under the shade of contemplations, fear and anxiety but went the next day and spoke out " I need to speak something to you " she nodded in affirmation. He continued " you look good and beautiful, what I mean, uhh...." She smiled and asked if it was. He continued, " can we become friends? " She reacted in an ambiguous way. She smiled a little more than earlier and went without saying anything. Her smile made him lost somewhere as he has got a new source to live with a new happiness. The next day he told her about the friendship's unanswered question, she remained silent. The boy asked her to join the tomorrow's party in which his all friends where invited, " it would be a pleasure for me ", but she talked about her schedule which seemed hectic but at the same time she said, " I am willing but probably me joining the party is rare, If I would be free from my work earlier... then sure." The rarity of her joining the party made him feel that it would go to surety, at least she approved. The same happened, as stated by lord Krishna the theory 'Yathartha', She came to the party and the decorations made by him felt the love, the atmosphere filled with fragrance and the party enchanted with decor. Her coming to the party brought changes and the boy felt the moment to be the happiest in his entire life. But not only he felt something strange, she too after seeing the beauty of decorations, found herself stepped at the junction of love and the blossomed garden of flowers plucked from heaven. But she indeed had her own work, family and routine, as we can clearly see ourselves in real life that the show must go on.......... nothing can be halted. And so, she went. The very next day he waited for her at same place where they met first. But something bizarre happened, she came weeping to him and said, " we can't meet like this now on " He got himself drowned in chaos. He became traumatic and heart sank into dizziness and lost the nerve to ask her the reason behind but uttered, " No problem, take care, Good Bye!" But every love story has phases of faith and distrust. He felt the same, he started losing his flavour of nature. Everything seemed insipid to his senses. He got drenched into the hands of illness. He started finding some ways to get her into contact and many a time asked her friends for just a meet with her. He gave her friends his own mobile number and told to give her saying that he is the one who cannot afford to see her wet eyelids. He waited for 3 continuous days for the ring in his phone but couldn't. He thought as if she is lost. But true love resides in a true heart whether it is full of sorrows or denials. She called her on the 4th day and said " Hello", her words he lost his way, got into the world of pleasing dreams of hallucinations. He stood to talk and with determination, he told the very common words of lover which is actually a gum jell between two hearts. But she took it offensively. But he continued with his soothing words, "you are the one who has made this naught into a crazy person, The one who has shown the vagabond a source of living for a cause, then how can't I, uhhh......" She then cut the phone with a little more laughter than those of earlier. But still the boy felt the dilemma of the reason for such expression. He then started reiterating the words, finding whether he could have spoken something wrong. He further couldn't get a single response from 76 calls he made that checked him into a sign of depression. Every single day without her voice made him cry as if years are passed in loneliness. But on the 6th Day he got a call from her and the voice came, " I'll come today, you please meet." Again, a very silly line of emotions and love which has no beginning and no end. The love which Harry was drowning deep burying the buoyancy, as per theory...but wait ....have I stated the name Harry, sorry readers....my apologies......the boy's name was 'Harry' and hers, 'Jasmine'. They called them with some nick names too but these were their actual identities as per UIDAI. Actually, I fled into the story of emotion which composes truly the hearts not the name ......but again it's my duty ....so, where were we? The love story continued now they called each other at the tuition class as it was their regular venue for meet, it was also untold...... and they again met there after the call that, " I'll come today to classes. You, please meet." Harry became happy and waited for the tuition classes. Then everything went very fine and expectedly well. Moreover, daily they started meeting, talking, sharing memories and knowing each other at the classes. The become so close that they started sharing food, you know what I mean. They both started living happily the lost smile was ocular on Harry's face with charm and expectations and the same happened with Jasmine. But I don't know why again an evil eye, which is known to be even dangerous than of a curse. Jasmine stopped coming to classes, and even their conservation came to a halt. But Harry till then was used to Jasmine as if she would have become an important daily chore. He again fell into a scenario of confusion, what to do and what not to....to whom could he share, neither his friends nor family but had a faith over lord Krishna that nothing goes in vain. Slowly and steadily, he made himself busy with his life, but a chunk of his soul was still crying for her voice. After few days, Harry suffered a stomach pain which seemed unnatural to him. Doctor said that the pain had to be operated, the situation was critical. This took his family into a shake of misfortune and gloom. Everyone started praying the Almighty for the recovery of Harry's health. The news somehow reached Jasmine. She became stunned and upset. She dialled him and asked his condition. Harry replied " Nothing Jasmine, it is just a small operation, I'll be fine, you take care." Jasmine boosted his confidence, "You are bold, nothing will happen to you, I know, know.... Everything is goanna be alright" But the inner conscience of Harry spoke, " where were you from those many days? Didn't you remember me? And now you are calling me when I want to forget you. I can't understand you. You are something .... leave it .... it would have been my mistake that I thought something with you actually I am not worth of it. Okay, I will tell you later." Jasmine got herself puzzled with the words of Harry. It was his care; it was his love actually which drove her to this moment of uncertainty. She went to temple, prayed for his well-being to Gods and Goddesses and returned home waiting, waiting and waiting until the Harry's call comes ... But there was neither calls nor conservations and thus the night passed by. When Harry got his consciousness, He was curious to know. He called up his mother and asked her whether somebody came to meet him. She replied, " Yes Harry, your teacher and your friends came. "Someone else, any girl." "No, no such girl." Then Harry searched for his mobile phone, he was astounded. It was brimming up with the messages and chats of love, missing and tears. There were 11 missed calls that made him call back to her.

She picked the phone up in the very first ring as if she was waiting anxiously for the call. But Harry was not in a situation to talk but he tried. She was silent the whole moment Harry was speaking like she would have come off her emotions. She replied, " You need to take rest, we will talk later". Now the talks and conversations remained of love, misses, but not of tears rather the future because they were thinking right what you're thinking right now. But Harry's life's happiness was intermittent, he was every shocked by fitful hoodoos and voodoos coming uninvitedly in his life. His happiness was just like the salt of the seas which resides in front of your eyes but difficult to obtain. Yes! Again after 15 days something happened. She made her last message to Harry stating, "our journey ends here, Harry, you go on your way, and I on my way. Further don't even dare to find me and no further questions.... take care. " Harry at this stage of life felt something usual that it happens again and again, meaning he didn't feel bad about that too much what he actually felt earlier. Thus, he replied, "Do whatever you wish, I won't object you, but mind it, you will surely feel someday the sense of my love when I will be far away, much far away from you." And she shifted her hometown to a new place and resumed her studies. Harry too got himself mingled with his studies in his institute, got good marks and aimed to become successful in future. But again, a day came when Harry's phone had a ring.... "Jasmine". But he didn't pick-up the call within a minute it was Jasmine again with call. "What the hell has happened to you? Why do you always try to disturb me? What is the matter?" Harry spoke rudely. Jasmine continued with her

Rosey voice, " I want to meet you right now, will you?" Harry reiterated, "No I have no vested interest in meeting you, just 'No' & 'No'." But she continued requesting, relentlessly, making Harry obsessed with his conflicting feelings.... He spoke "Okay!". It was his love may be that really has no space for the logics and reasoning .... He went and meet her. Their meet again was an adventurous takeover for Harry down the lane. But that was observed by Jasmine's family. Yes, their meet didn't remain secret actually what they thought. She said, "Harry, please don't reveal this meet to anyone. This must be confidential between us", and she went to her home. After 2 days, it was a ring on Harry's cell phone. It was neither his friends or family nor Jasmine......an unknown number. He picked up the phone, "Hello! are you Harry? If yes, can you please come to xxx place, I wanna meet you". He went without questioning or knowing anything about him. After reaching that place xxx, he got to know that, it was her brother, Jasmine's brother. But he asked it a very usual and friendly way, "Hi! what's the matter, why have you called me?" He asked, " from how many days have you been in contact with Jasmine and why?......and which sort of relationship do you have with her? Harry said causally, "No, we meet each other at tuition classes and now we are .... just friends and nothing else". "Then why the fuck have you meet her elsewhere than the tuition.... 2 days back", he asked in a derogatory manner. "No brother, it isn't the actual matter, might have been mistaken or something because it isn't the truth" "Ohno, it means you won't speak. Okay, I will explain...... The one whom you met at the place has disclosed your name and also told that you asked her force fully come to the very place for a secret meet which she repeatedly denied, "her brother spoke with the piercing words. Now, not only I, and Harry can feel the pain, but the condition of harry at the moment. He was dumbstruck as if something has been chocked in his throat & hard leading his every cell of his body go insensate. But he had a great faith over his love. He asked her brother to make her a call and asked if the whole incident is true. He called her, jasmine boldly replied, "yes it him, harry, who empathetic force me for the secret meet which I didn't want... Again, a shock of thunder and grief, which harry was not feeling for the first time, but it was the most intensified because it was not only a pain of separation due to denial but also the deceive, a cheat which unexpectedly came from an unexpected individual.

He was lost into thoughts...." I did a grave mistake in understanding the person........again a very big faults in my life". Harry was insulted with no reason and logic with a very bad tag name. But he wanted always to just wash off the memories and so he never expressed or tried to prove himself correct.... He never reacted. He left everything as a very bad night- mare and started accepting the true vibes of lord Krishna about 'Yathartha'. Now, Harry had completed his intermediate and was planning for a college to join, a college very far away his home town where he could spend his life happily and peacefully. And the family got some college away and still with no confusion of thoughts and peace to become successful. But if the life has already surrendered for someone's unluck and ill fate, then even God finds it difficult to unravel it. Harry's train was at 6:30 AM and he had already packed up his bags and baggage's early evening for a good long sleep before travel. But Jasmine was still weeping under her sheath of mistakes, the cry which only she suffered by the course of time concealing from other's actually she was repenting over her past, her past with Harry.... from beginning till end, but she didn't want to end with such a note .... she was wondering over the moving of Harry," He didn't utter a single word against me", even after his deep malign. She called on Harry's friend's cell phone at 1 AM and asked him, "Is there someone in Harry's life? Will he forgive me?". He replied, "I don't know anything about him and now a day's, I even don't know where he is", so, she called on Harry's mobile, but he didn't pick up .... because he didn't want himself to be tangled with her anymore. She made 14 missed calls to Harry. After waking early, Harry made himself fresher and was taken aback after seeing the 14 missed calls and 2 SMS from some unknown number. He didn't care to much as he was hurrying for the train. He took his bags and essentially and moved for catching his train on time ... On the way, He called backed on the mobile number of so called 'unknown number' and was bewildered after hearing Jasmine's voice "How are you? Where are you?" Harry knew the consequences," hang up the call, I don't have time to tell you in fact I don't wanna tell you and what the hell has made you call at sudden to me after the whole 1 year. Again, don't even dare to tell a lie" She replied," Actually, even I don't have to talk to you, I just want to meet you". Harry said rudely "Mrs, I am running out of time, I have no time for these bullshits, Bye!" She again called him and started weeping, "please Harry, there is goanna be no mistake. Please meet me before you go elsewhere". Harry couldn't control his emotion right there; he frosted heart melted listening her stammered weeping voice. He collected his courage and spoke," I would have met you, Jasmine but the time is very less. In fact, my train is at 6:30AM". Jasmine was silent meanwhile because she wanted to listen something more. "Jasmine, do you remember what I told you year back, you will surely feel the sense of my love when I will be far away. And now I am going to my college, very-very far away ". Jasmine broke into tears, her voice got more stammered repenting over her deeds, "my apologies, please let me meet you last time ever". Harry knew that she is not going to stop until he resolves the matter with a full stop. He said, "okay then, you're left with 20 minutes, it's 16:10 now, if you can come to the station its well and good, otherwise...." Jasmine hurried up, she put her beat behind to reach station in time, harshly did she left home but it was almost impossible to reach within 20 minutes of time. But it's still the almighty judged the love to be true and the train got late by 10 minutes, as a miracle.... Harry was still hopeless of meeting her but when they saw each other after a long search she ran and hugged themselves.... wow! Really a very good scene of love. Jasmine wept her heart out asking harry for the forgiveness with all she called. Harry, he was noble and generous, he replied, "I am not angry, I don't have any malice or ill will, then for what are you asking my forgiveness ". Her eyes glowed, she wiped her tears and spoke," you took the whole blame on yourself, even it wasn't your fault. You lied for me and did bear the sorrows. I remained sleepless seeing your human attitude. If today I wouldn't have come for apologise, I might have never forgiven myself entire life". Harry said, "well, I have never considered that matter. You did whatever you liked, for yourself and I did what I liked for myself". She could get what harry started and started playing with the thought of the words. Harry continued, "you", for your happiness, defamed me, slandered my image in front of everyone. But I for your happiness only got slandered with no ill will in my heart. That is the difference, a difference of living for self, a difference of philanthropy, selfish and selfless". She actually understood this buried pain echoing in an abyss pit of grief. She begged "please, love me like you did earlier, I am requesting " Harry obstinately said, "Now, I am not in such a condition to love anybody, my heart and soul further do not want to be used of cheats and deceives. I can't trust anyone now, but for you, I would treat you as a good person, for me nothing…. no more expectations." Jasmine reiterated," but want to see our future, together till the doom's day your presence in my life." Harry didn't care more, he started hurrying for the train, "I'm getting late and wait since you're come here, please take this is the thing I keep near to my heart and be happy enjoy, no more regrets and specially no weeping, keep your tear, don't let it out, it may have some significance later" these last words of Harry made her happy but at the same time her dreams for a life time with him got vanished into hazy fog mistakes. Harry departed…… But still Harry's departure from the soul of Jasmine seemed impossible she tried every means and their relationship which existed once because it is said if there's a possibility of 0.001% even, one must try. But the storms of struggles and sufferings resided inside Harry, he became stubborn not to believe her at any cost. Jasmine had a pinch of many questions……," why? Why doesn't he talk to me proper, why always doe she talk to me like this" Jasmine persistently provoked Harry not to disclose their secret convection. But Harry insisted not to tell her. He continuously ignored her and begged for let him being alone for few days. So, Jasmine didn't call him for many days. After a long period, she called him and spoke, "listen Harry, I am in urgency of some amount of money, but the sum is large. I will repay it to you for sure." Obsessed of her, Harry told, "I can't help you out Mrs; sorry." "At least you can try, try it for me", she insisted Harry in an offensive way, "sorry, I can't …. Bye!" Again, Jasmine made him a call after 3 days. "Please Harry! Please, you are my only last expectation. It is utterly urgent at least if not for me, then for our love, I beg you, Harry." Harry tried to ignore her but at the same time, it was not his love actually, it was his humanity, generosity and selflessness which made him help her. She was very grateful for his help and said, "Thank you, Harry you did and have been doing these many things for me, with no question and never asked anything from me except love. Why? What is there inside you which makes you so humane?" Harry replied, "See Jasmine, love doesn't exist for self-greed and ego. It exists for happiness and satisfaction which the lovers want to see in them. It is never materialistic because it is just a feeling, an emotion of affection....". " And these helps, are actually not for favouring you as a beneficiary, it is just a human thing, which our fore fathers taught us " Jasmine was very happy and with a smile, " you are very good. You are the person selfless to attitude. I feel myself unfortunate, that I couldn't win you love, and even I don't deserve it for seal. And you were right love between us is just a play of distance and at this juncture, when I am so, so far away from you, I feel your love, your emotions and your affection. Harry again found himself in a scenario of confusion. He was not able to judge anything at the moment as if someone has buried him between the devil and the deep blue sea but the memories still resided in his mind without uttering a single word …… He hanged up the phone. Jasmine tried every pillar to post to talk and convince Harry of her love. To re-begin their talks and be a part of his life but harry kept on ignoring her many a time. But tired of this harry once text, "I don't want my life to again fall into the middle of thick, deep and dense red wood forest where every relationship has a tax to be paid off and where one drives himself away from family, friends and success". " I would have loved you, but condition of my heart makes one cry please, let me love my own life, your love always pulls me to the darkness. Again listen, I don't have any courage left to fight for you and you keep defaming me proving me a liar. You made the life of a happy person an inferno full of aghast and suffering. You made him loss of realties. He is dead for you " Jasmine replied in text, " I am sorry. I feel bad after knowing your condition, fighting for life. It seems you would never forgive me, no issues but, I will try my best to tell you whether you like it or not because I don't want you to be lost again. You are my well-wishers. If the almighty doesn't want our relationship in future, it's no matter, I will be talking to you till the last breath of my life" Harry didn't reply after seeing these messages because he understood the self-aggrandized love of her. It remained un replied. Again after 2 days, Harry's phone had a ring. " Why the hell are you bullying me from those many days' what shit have I done to you. I am not goanna share you at any cost. It is going to results you very bad, I am saying" Harry was bewildered after those words touching his eardrum, it was Jasmine on the phone. He started wondering the muck she told him, the reason? The Couse?, The anger ? Why? Why again?? Because offended, he called Jasmine on phone and asked her the reason behind, " you made your friend call me, disturbing me many a times and he used such vulgar words that I can't express. You have only done this I know". Harry got astounded, he asked his identity to Jasmine. Jasmine replied, " It was Jazz who called me, disturbing me too much and told your name, Harry who told him to do so it will cost you Harry, you have played with my sentiments". She then hanged up the phone. Before proceeding further, I want my readers to be introduced about Jazz, who he is and why he did like that. I'll take you to the flashback, an incident of 2015, jazz and harry were very good friend. True to everything. They spent time with each other wandering, playing, studies and everything they had. They used to share everything they had whether it is eyeglasses or laptop and smartphone everything was going very fine and good in their lovely friendship. But it is told that if you are getting two golden tickets for your dream come true, you need to decide one of them. The same happened with harry, Jasmine came in his life and he started spending comparatively more time with Jasmine, webbed in the love, he gave almost no concerns to jazz and his inclination to her got a greater proximity that was enough far jazz to feel bad and revengeful. Deranged from the love between harry and Jasmine, jazz got enraged for the revenge, a revenge to end to end up their love story. Jazz secretly took out the phone number of Jasmine from Harry's mobile. He called Jasmine by his own number and addressed her heavenly, full of vulgar words with abuses and claims and casted the name of Harry for this call. Harry was unknown of this untold fact but it is rightly said, even if the day is full of merriment and happiness, but the fate is wretched, then the life gears up into the infernos full of purgatories and the cause remains upon your shoulder itself. Jasmine on the other side was frustrated and announced of the thing. "The one who constantly devoted his eternal life, to get one, to get my love has today when I don't want to lose him, denied it, renounced our relationship with old page of nostalgia". Then Jasmine also thought of a revenge, the one who couldn't be mine, can't be anyone else's. There started torturing Harry, "Why you did it? What was the reason behind?". Harry had nothing to reply at the moment, He made many a call to jazz but was resulted with ' no reply'. And something very miserable happened. Jasmine told her whole family about that call of abuses and claims of which Harry was responsible. The very next day, the whole family of Jasmine reached Harry's home and started revealing their stories and particularly that phone call. They started claiming, " Harry has been trying to defame Jasmine and has showered her with abuses and slandered her execrably. The false claims and assertion made Harry astounded and shocked totally. He tolerated all the accusations and said no single word. He didn't even try to prove himself correct at any juncture and came back quiets. Harry was very much evident and confident of the fact that if he could have spilled the beans of Jasmine, every pressure she gave, every help she took, every dream she had with him etc, then each family members of Jasmine would have lost the courage of to live with their heads-up in society, to live with respect and glory...... It all would have been lost and reciprocatively Jasmine would have also suffered tortures, blames, curses, ill - treatment with great persecution. But Harry did not do anything just for humanity and compassion. He didn't even want the story to continue again with tantrums and paroxysm. And so, he bluntly took all the blames over his own head. Harry's life was shattered into little fragments of cheats and deceives filled with agony of revenge. Harry's family started loathing him, cursing him, blaming him unconditionally. At that moment, he was left with nothing but the milieu of traduces and libels. They were not standing for him at this labyrinth. Now Harry was repenting, remorseful of his own philanthropic attitude he had with her, which took his life into the scenario of denials and forbids. "Why did I say lies for her? For her well-being. It's all my fault which consequently affect my life. The life which was happier and merrier before, with my parents, with my family.... I did a blunder, it's true." The condition of Harry got deteriorated day by day. He got physically and mentally disturbed. Desperate from the reality, he made his own world, lost in it, trying to find some source of pleasure, delight and contentment. Living aloof, his life got submerged with memories into a dead pit of hell. Harry was a liar in everyone's eyes.... Philosophers say," a love story ends with a happy note." But hard to swallow my friends .... "His happy notes ended with a love story."

.... The End........